EXIT THE KING

A PLAY BY

FELICITY FAIR THOMPSON

This play was first shown on the Isle of Wight in three performances at the Ventnor Fringe Festival 2017 as an historical one act monologue for a single actor, and then again on 29th January 2018 at Carisbrooke Castle in the Great Hall in the Museum.
It has been re-written here with a supporting character.

Wight Diamond Press
39 Ranelagh Road
Sandown, IW PO36 8NT

ISBN 978-1-78955-211-9

www.wightdiamondpress.com

29th January 1649

The axe is sharp and ready! Tomorrow morning King Charles I will die! The Parliamentarians have won. Through this long night, the King thinks back across the events that led to this end. His friend Sir John Oglander on the Isle of Wight has sent his trusted manservant, young Vivas, to keep Charles company in his last hours.

The King remembers his childhood in Scotland, his father's accession to the English throne, his own coronation, his family. After his final year imprisoned at Carisbrooke Castle on the Isle of Wight, Charles I considers how many things have happened since he came to the throne - rebellion in Ireland, quarrels over religion and money, the Scots fighting over the border, the parliamentary disagreements, the political uprisings, and the long Civil War...

Outside the window in Whitehall, the scaffold waits.

EXIT THE KING

CHARLES I, forty-nine, has a pronounced stammer on some occasions when he is emotional. At those times his neck and jaw muscles contract. Used only at moments where it matters - and for ease of reading, only particularly pointed out on some pages.

Sir John Oglander, a Royalist friend and supporter on the Isle of Wight has sent his trusted servant VIVAS to keep the King company in his final hours, to listen. CHARLES sometimes directs his conversation at VIVAS, but most of the time it is to us all or to himself that CHARLES is talking, in spoken recollection.

EXIT THE KING

Setting: Night. A room in Whitehall. 29th January 1649.
Hanging Portraits: Mary Queen of Scots, James I, Queen Elizabeth I
On a round table: The bible. A feather pen. A scroll of paper. An ornate wine glass. The King's hat. A walking cane leans against a grand chair.

ACT I

VIVAS enters and places a wine flagon on the table. He retreats to downstage right, sits on the ground, and huddles under his cloak.

CHARLES enters upstage right, pulling his cloak closer round him. He goes to the table, picks up the wine flagon and examines the label. He looks across at Vivas.

CHARLES
How kind of dear Sir John Oglander to send this. And <u>you</u> to keep me company this night.

He pours a little wine into a glass. Tastes it.
Excellent!

He pours more wine into his glass.
Have you come far?

VIVAS
From the Island, Sire.

CHARLES
Of course. Isle of Wight to Whitehall.

VIVAS
Two long days travel.

CHARLES
Well, keep your cloak about you – these are cold rooms.
Takes a long slow sip of wine.
This is the night for reflection. For memories.

He turns one quarter to stage right, looks at the picture…
That's my grandmama, Mary - the Queen of the Scots.
Turning across to the next picture – raises his glass.
James - my father. S-s-sixth of Scotland. First of England.
Turns to the last picture.
And the English Queen, Elizabeth. There are paintings of her - everywhere…

Then he turns back to Vivas.
Pale. Pale white skin. Thin crimson lips.
(flouncing to demonstrate) Those high stiff collars.
And jewellery. So much jewellery. Such extravagance!
Look at me. I dress simply. I don't waste money.

(dreamily to himself) I remember the warmth of Scottish firesides when I was a child. The smell of burning wood... Bagpipes... My older brother Henry leading me by the hand through the halls. He knows where we have to go, the things we must do... I can hear us whispering... And the echoes of our footsteps on the stone floors...
Takes another sip of wine, remembering.

Looks up urgently at the audience, agitated.
But then suddenly people are hurrying. There's noise. Uproar. Bowing. Packing. Horses in the courtyard. My brother says there are Courtiers come. Important people from London. Red boxes. 'Quick, this way,' Henry says. 'Hurry!'
I was just three years old, but I remember it so well. And they all left for London without me! My brother. The gentlemen of the bedchambers. My mother.
For a year, a whole year, I stayed with Lord Flyvie and his family. I was sickly and found walking difficult. And he complained about me all the time: 'The child can no' walk! The child can no' talk!'

I don't remember my journey to London. I was only four. Maybe I slept.
I remember all the c-clamour in the London streets. The cheering. The shouting. In Westminster. Here in Whitehall. My father is K-K...

I am the King's <u>second</u> son. The small child in this new court. They look at my brother Henry. They talk to my sister Elizabeth. Nobody looks at me. Nobody talks to me.

I have constant maladies. No one comforts me.
Palaces are such isolated, empty places.
(Angrily) I always stand alone!

Turning to Vivas.
Will you take my dog with you when you leave? My little spaniel. She needs...

Vivas nods.

CHARLES
(relaxing a little)
Thank you. Treat her well. She has been a sweet friend.

He *takes a comforting sip of wine and puts the glass down on the table.*

To Vivas.
When we lived here in Westminster as a family, my father escaped being murdered. Do you remember it? The gunpowder plot - sixteen hundred and five?
The plotters dug tunnels. Crept through under our Palace with explosives. Guy Fawkes - he was the Englishman who hated the Scots - hated my father.
And Robert Catesby. Everard Digby. Evil friends. Traitors.

Speaking out into the theatre.
We were all locked down, the whole family. All in different parts of the palace. My sister Elizabeth was whisked off to Coventry - the traitors might capture her for their cause. Guards! Questions! Constant surveillance!

Someone with me every moment.
Soldiers watching at every window, every door.
Some of the plotters were shot as they escaped. The others were drawn on a hurdle. And hanged. I saw their entrails taken out and burnt before their eyes. It was the talk of the court. Digby's heart was plucked out and held up before he died. The heart of a traitor! Behold! He was executed on – on... (*Sudden agitation on his face)* On the thirtieth of January.

Planning to kill the King, they were. Treason! That's treason! It's treason!
When my father was King, the plotters died. Now I am King, where are the plotters? Running the country!
...In the name of God!

Picks up the bible and holds it up.
My father's Bible. The King James Bible!

Presses the bible to his chest, and looks out into the audience, suddenly emotional.

My children. What will happen to my children?
Beware my sweet son. Tomorrow they will cut off thy father's head. They will cut off your brothers' heads too when they can catch them.
They will cut off your head at the last. Do not - do not be made a king by them.
And you, my Elizabeth, remember all I've told you. Keep your faith in the Protestant religion. You tell your dear

mother my thoughts never strayed. My love will be the same to the last.

He stands silent and absolutely still for a moment.
Then he goes to the table and puts the bible down, but he leans on it for support.
He looks up suddenly.

Let me see Henry! I want to see my brother! Let me see him! I stand outside the door to his bedchamber crying. Let me see him!
He is not well, they say. Go away, child.
They will not let me in. He has the fever, they say.
And then he's gone! Typhoid!
I'm twelve. Suddenly I'm heir to the throne. I must become the future King the country expects.
Study. S..s...speak in p...p..ublic.
God, have I not tried?

(Urgently looking at Vivas and thumping the bible)
You'll never speak of what you've heard. Not to a soul! Ever! You swear on your life?

VIVAS
I swear, Sire. Never.

(CHARLES smiles)
You are a good listener.

He relaxes a little, takes off the cloak and hangs it over the chair.
In the great halls, everyone talked about my sister Elizabeth. They all said how beautiful she was. They heard my stammer and said how beautiful my older sister was. She married a prince from the German Royal family. Prince Frederick, Elector Palatine. Good title!
He was a staunch Protestant. My mother was thrilled. *(Acting the part)* 'Frederick,' says my mother, 'is a very fortunate man marrying into the English Royal blood line. And Charles,' she says, 'you will soon have German cousins.'

He lifts the flagon and pours a little more wine.

Holds up the glass.
On summer evenings we had Command Performances - plays performed at Court. And more often, once the Globe theatre burned down. The Tempest. A Winter's Tale. On that night, Hamlet. It was in the Great Hall *(indicating these surroundings)* - like this.
To Vivas.
How old are you?

VIVAS
Nearly seventeen, Sire.

CHARLES
Sixteen, sixteen. My sixteenth birthday. That was the first time I drank too much wine.

He takes a sip of wine with remembered pleasure.

George Villiers, Duke of Buckingham, was there – standing too close to my father. As usual. He was my father's favourite at Court. Even more than that. Touching my father's arm. Whispering to him!

He lifts the glass aggressively.

And he turned and laughed at me. Laughed at my h-h-hesitation. In front of them all! In front of all the gentlemen of the Court – and the actors!
'All this study, he says, now you are your father's h-h-h-heir? Think you will outshine H-h-henry?'
I could not hold back my fury. I put my fingers round the water fountain spout and aimed the spray at Buckingham.
(shouting now) Don't instruct me on my duty! You will not be <u>my</u> favourite. We have a history that goes back centuries. You are just the disappointing son of minor gentleman!
He throws the contents of the wine glass across the stage. Vivas ducks.

CHARLES
I soaked him through!
Even my father laughed.

Charles smiles and lifts the glass to his lips. He is surprised to find it empty.
He moves back to the table and pours more wine into the glass. He takes a good sip.

To Vivas.
What's your name?

VIVAS
Vivas. My name is Vivas, Sire.

CHARLES
A name bestowed on you to bring good luck?

VIVAS (surprised)
Yes, Sire.

CHARLES
Spanish?
(*Vivas nods enthusiastically*)

Secretly Buckingham and I went to Spain to meet the Spanish princess. My father wanted me to marry her! But we discovered to wed her I had to convert to c-c-Catholicism and change English laws to suit the Spanish negotiators! Buckingham and I spent some time there. But as soon as I was safely on the ship for home, we said - <u>never!</u> <u>Never!</u> <u>Never!</u> There's a nice monument in Portsmouth to my return!
But the Spanish do live well. Beautiful palaces. Beautiful paintings…

Henrietta was the youngest daughter of King Henri IV of France. Her brother was the new French King - Louis XIII. I had never met her even in my time abroad, but we might build an alliance with France if I married <u>her</u>. Buckingham helped me draw up a treaty to protect her religious rights - a secret document Parliament didn't know about. In it I promised to suspend the laws here against Catholics.

Charles slowly pulls the robe from the grand chair and puts it on with great care and grandeur. He takes up his cane and faces the audience.

March. Sixteen twenty-five.
My father died in his sleep last night. The K-K-King is dead.
Long live the King.

He lifts his head to smell the air.
A strange smell, incense. And the anointing oil - the Holy Spirit sanctifying the King unto God.
King Charles the First. By the glory of God, I had come to the throne of the Three Kingdoms.
George Villiers, The Duke of Buckingham knelt to kiss my hand. 'You will be a good King,' he said. 'Better than your brother.'

Charles moves the cloak on him to be less formal - undoes the cord and throws one side back over his shoulder.

But back to marriage.
(To Vivas)
A religious man, are you?
No! Don't answer. We won't discuss that tonight. There's nothing but trouble in religious difference.
So - a Catholic princess married the Protestant King!

Henrietta and I were wed by proxy with special dispensation from the Pope. She in France. Myself in England.
And of course, Parliament - they all objected to her – well, Pym and his Puritan friends.
I'm the King! I was trying to do the right thing for the country. I could have married the Spanish girl. Instead I married the French princess to make an alliance with France – our two countries standing strong together against Spain. Better together they say.
My friend Buckingham - he had become my friend - but he didn't like her either.
The Anglican Bishops all hated her. They said the marriage would undermine the Church of England. Henrietta was not permitted at the coronation. If she had been here in England, the doors of Westminster would have been closed to her. It is an Anglican ceremony.

A whole year on - and I still hadn't met her.

He abandons the cloak and the cane and returns them to the chair. He loosens his collar - and just for one second feels his throat.

When Henrietta finally arrived, we were married formally at Canterbury.
Buckingham still didn't like her!
I remember it was impossible to see her! She was surrounded by Roman Catholic servants who only spoke French! Buckingham agreed with me. Why were they

here? I could not afford them! I sent them back to France! She kept just her chaplain and two ladies.

He pours a glass of wine, entwines his arm to make a loving cup of it, then suddenly he pulls out of that and holds the glass high.

Nine months later our firstborn was christened Charles James, Prince of Wales. He died on the very day of his birth.

Vivas crosses himself.

CHARLES
In France Henrietta's brother was at war with the Protestant Huguenots. Parliament wanted me to send troops to fight on the Protestant side. How could I do that? Upset my new Catholic wife? Undermine Louis, the King of France? My new brother in law? Instead I sent men to fight for <u>him</u>! I sent Buckingham with them, but the men wouldn't fight! They abandoned their weapons and deserted Buckingham. They dispersed into the French countryside. How dare they?

Because of it, the House of Commons - Pym and his friends, started arguing with <u>me</u>.
I am their King. God's anointed King! They should obey me. I say if we go to war. If we make peace. I draft the laws. I appoint senior advisors. I summon Parliament.

They said they didn't trust me with money! Spain was making threats, but Pym and his friends wouldn't grant the funds for any naval encounters.
What about the tax money? That should have been allocated to the war effort. The Royal coffers were empty. Parliament should have given me the tax money I was entitled to.
Certain politicians I just couldn't deal with! Sir John Elliot - he said he would impeach Buckingham! I imprisoned Elliot. Parliament demanded Elliot's release. They said I must dismiss Buckingham.

VIVAS
Dismiss your friend?

CHARLES lifts the paper scroll as if it is the Mace.
I dismissed Parliament! I would rule without them.
So to raise finance, I sold knighthoods. I took cash for honours! And I raised taxes.

And Buckingham argued for me in the House of Commons. That's why I had such affection for him. A friend of the family, he served me loyally. I trusted him. But his military expeditions <u>did</u> go wrong. He lost four thousand men in one skirmish with the French! The wars cost me dear. And Buckingham made such tactical errors.

He unrolls the scroll.
For the good of the country's finances, and with God's grace, I recalled Parliament to request funds. But they had drawn up a Petition of Rights against me! They wished to

restrain my power. Their King! I must promise - promise - no import duty will be raised in the future without specific parliamentary grant!
(Holds up the scroll)
Look! Look! No man shall be forced to pay tax or gift money or loan without the consent of Parliament!
No freeman shall be imprisoned without reason!
No man will be forced to house soldiers or sailors unless he keeps an inn and is paid!
Their consent to raise taxes? And just where would I house my troops?
It costs money to run a country! Where do they think it comes from?
'What watch the King keeps to maintain the peace.'

He shrugs, picks up the pen and signs with a flourish.
I granted this by 'my grace'. Not forced by them. Just a signature. Look! Charles!
Charles Rex! Sixteen twenty-eight.

He rolls the paper scroll, puts it down. Walks round the table to the other side and concentrates on pouring a little more wine into the glass on the table.
He looks up at VIVAS, pleased.
They granted me all monies owing. But they were still after Buckingham. And now there was a new voice in the House. Oliver Cromwell. He's a real Puritan. I brought him before the courts and fined him because he wouldn't pay for a knighthood. All men with land of value had to purchase this honour. Then Pym wouldn't pay either.

I decide all tax. I appoint who I choose. I say if we go to war. I make peace. It is my prerogative to rule. I know what the country needs. I am God's anointed King.
He picks up the glass of wine.

Pause.

VIVAS
And Buckingham?

CHARLES
Buckingham was killed by some army officer in the Greyhound Public House in Portsmouth. My father's friend. Mine too. A loyal man. I could not bear the national rejoicing.

He takes a sip of wine. Straightens up. He's the King.
He nods towards VIVAS.
So I dissolved my Parliament again. They were asking too much of me. Arguing. Never deferring. I could not have such disagreement. I would rule alone... over -
'This earth of majesty, this seat of Mars,
This other Eden, demi paradise,
This precious stone set in a silver sea,
This blessed plot, this earth, this realm, this England...'

And Ireland!
And Scotland!

He leans forward to confide in us, - it is a secret he's telling us.
I was suddenly having long conversations with Henrietta.

We were both the children of Kings.
'Yes, Charles,' she said, 'though I was barely a year old when my father was murdered on a French street. Knifed! What if you were murdered by these Puritans? I want you alive and strong.'
Such an interesting woman. We had more in common than I first realised.

VIVAS
The Catholic. The French princess.

CHARLES
The Queen! She began to assist me in the day-to-day running of affairs. She was not liked of course. She is Catholic. She is a foreigner. She is a woman.
Dear Henrietta. She has such strong faith. She practices it openly - and with such fervour. The Carmelite nuns taught her so much when she was a child. That year, to please her, I invited the Papal Envoy to discuss the possibility of re-uniting the English church with Rome. *(pleased)* That so annoyed Pym and his Protestant friends!

CHARLES returns to the table and puts down the glass. He's in charge.

When you are God's King, Parliament does not need to sit.
I rule. I am the King!
…I know
'Tis not the balm, the sceptre, and the ball,
The sword, the mace, the crown im…im…imperial…
imperial.'

It's leading the country!

I so enjoy Will Shakespeare's plays. They are printed now of course.
KING JOHN... HENRY THE FIFTH.
KING CHARLES THE FIRST. I could have been a play!

VIVAS clasps his hands together in delight.

CHARLES
And I kept perfect order! I used my Star Chamber to prosecute my opponents. My Court sat in secret, with no indictments, no right of appeal. No juries. No witnesses. I suppressed all opposition to my policies. And I made <u>peace</u> with Spain and France.
Without Parliament I could raise income any way I wanted. Forced loans. Import duties. Selling commercial monopolies - now there's a good one: I granted just <u>one</u> businessman the right to sell bricks, or soap, or salt. *(Charles clasps his hands together gleefully)* I acquired a new source of income too. Ship money! By law the Crown is bound to build ships in preparation for war. We were not at war of course, but I could be preparing! Keeping this blessed Isle safe. The County Sheriffs wrote to me saying they were over-burdened with taxes - but all tax payers must pay ship tax and it must come direct to the crown. Oliver Cromwell's cousin John Hampden defied me. He refused to pay it. 'If the King be no Papist, then his friends are, and his family. The King is a tyrant!' Papist? Tyrant? The law courts upheld my legal right. Quite right too! Now

I could maintain an army. Maintain my position. I certainly did not need Pym. Or Cromwell. Or his cousin!

VIVAS
You had no need of Parliament, Sire!

CHARLES
No! And trade and commerce prospered. My finances were sound.
I had excellent advisors - Thomas Wentworth, the Earl of Strafford, for one. He was anti-royalist but he had come over to my side. I made him Lord President of the Council of the North. And in Ireland he encouraged our Protestants to settle on Catholic land. He has tripled the taxes there. I really like him. He wields a firm hand.

It was a golden age. I commissioned portraits of me. Rubens. Van Dyke. My people could see in my true colours.

I'm God's anointed King. Through devout prayer I know what's right. The country needs to be on a sound financial footing. The King needs money. To defend the realm. To make right and proper decisions for his people. To uphold the law. To rule in God's name.

He lifts the Bible.
I appointed my friend and supporter William Laud as Archbishop of Canterbury. He wanted strict religious conformity across my Three Kingdoms. The Church of England and the Church of Ireland were brought together

by the ancient Church Fathers. The Anglican way is recorded in Magna Carta.
(directly to Vivas)
You've read that, haven't you?

Vivas draws back - he hasn't read it.

CHARLES
And I was crowned north of the border! Charles III of Scotland!
June - that was the month - mid summer, sixteen thirty-three, at the Church of the Holy Rood in Edinburgh. At my insistence, and of course my Bishops agreed, for my anointing and my crowning, the true Anglican ceremonial was used.
I paraded from the Castle down the Royal Mile with my Van Dyke royal portrait leading the procession. The fountains flowed with red wine. Such a bonnie do!

I commissioned a beautiful new prayer book for Scotland. But there were riots in the churches when the book was read. Commoners wielding sticks and stones - and cricket bats! And then the Scots as a nation rose up against me! 'We will no' accept what England sends us,' the Presbyterians said.
England? England? I am <u>their</u> King!
The English worship is the only true way. God knows I am right, but the Scots would not have it. The Marquis of Montrose, and one of those wild <u>Campbells,</u> took up arms and marched into England.

The Earl of Strafford gathered twenty thousand men for me, and the money to fund them, but they could not hold the Scots back. Durham and Northumberland were lost.
'We will no' have English Bishops,' says Montrose. 'We have abolished your prayer book.'
Bastard!
Always, always - it's religion and borders...
Eleven years of calm and then…
'Oh Scotland... Scotland.'

He puts the Bible down sharply.
They demanded I must not to interfere with religion in Scotland. And they wanted compensation or they would leave their army in England. £40,000 a month!

VIVAS
A month?

CHARLES
I had no choice but recall Parliament to request funds. John Pym and his Puritan friends thought it was all some Catholic plot - and then <u>they</u> wanted conditions set!
They said they would trade money for power - that I may not do as I wish - that I was bound to do as they said.
Cromwell even formed his own 'model' army to fight me!

(speaking out into the theatre)
I woke at night thinking of the Earl of Strafford, and all he had done for me in Ireland and up north. He raised money for me. Fought for me. And William Laud - my Archbishop of Canterbury - he was in trouble with

Cromwell and Pym for replacing the wooden communion tables in churches with stone alters! Both these friends of mine were to be executed.

He unrolls the scroll. He picks up the feather pen.
If I wanted Parliament to support me against the Scots, I had to sign the two death warrants. *(Angrily)* Money in exchange for friends? To fight off the King's enemies? To fund a war on the Scottish border?

He signs, then rolls the scroll slowly. He pours more wine for himself - he holds the glass but does not drink yet.
Parliament was subverting my authority. Bastards like John Pym. War mongers like Oliver Cromwell.

Henrietta tried to raise finance from English Catholics for our cause. And then Parliament wanted to impeach her! Impeach the Queen!
I made the decision to take Henrietta and the princes to Harwich. Send them to Europe.
(wistfully) When they had sailed, I rode along the cliff top. My men were screaming at me: 'Come back! Sire! Come back! Cromwell's army is barely ten miles away!' I rode on, keeping the ship in sight until the last white sail had vanished.

Now he does take a sip from the wine glass.
I'm sure it was Pym and his friends, Hampton, Haselrig, Strode and Hollis who urged the Scots to invade England. And then they turned all London against me. There were riots in the streets. It was dangerous. I would not have it!

Once my family was safe, I made the unprecedented decision to storm the House of Commons. I took four hundred fighting men armed with muskets and swords and we burst through the Royal Gate and into the Commons Chamber. There was such shouting and blaspheming! But Pym and his four friends were gone! I'm sure they'd slipped out to the river. Escaped by boat.
I held back my fury and sat calmly in the Speaker's Chair.
So the birds have flown? Tell me where they are!
Speaker Lenthall fell on his knees. 'May it please your Majesty…'
(furiously) May it please me?
'May it please your Majesty, I have neither eyes to see, nor tongue to speak in this place, unless the House is pleased to direct me.'

Charles snarls with fury - and swallows down the wine that is left in the glass.
The threat to me was within the House. The real threat was Parliament!

He looks out into the audience.
If your power is taken from you, your crown threatened, would you run? Or turn and fight?

Pause

To the west I joined my Army of Royalist supporters. Our first attack to regain London got as far as Turnham Green, but we were forced back - and back again, when we attacked Reading.

Now the Scots were fighting alongside Cromwell's army in Newark and York.
And all those ships I built? The Navy sided with Parliament!
From Nottingham I put out the call. All Royalist men, take up arms!
I brought men back from Ireland to fight the cause. And then - then I was accused of some Catholic Conspiracy!
Total Civil War had broken out. Oh God!

He stares for a moment or two into space.

VIVAS
So much fighting? Oh, Sire!

CHARLES
Nearly a year of fighting went by. The war raged on. And now there was rebellion in Ulster too.

He comes back from thought, brighter.
My dear Henrietta landed in Yorkshire bringing troops from Europe to join the Royalist forces. She stayed with the Earl of Newcastle in York. *(cheerfully)* Persuaded by her, Cholmley delivered Scarborough Castle to our side. We were winning hearts and minds.

VIVAS sits forward eagerly.

CHARLES
The Queen sent me a message. 'Her She-Majesty Generalissima' will meet you with her army near Oxford

and together we will march triumphantly into the city. My dear Henrietta! We raised the Royal Standard once more over Nottingham.

VIVAS punches the air.

CHARLES
Like RICHARD THE SECOND: I wept 'for joy to stand upon my kingdom once again...'

Best of all - now we had the support of the Irish! We bought them off and they signed a peace agreement with my Royalists.

VIVAS
And the Scots?

CHARLES puts the wine glass down, holds it with two hands and looks into it for a few seconds, like a crystal ball.
When he looks up at Vivas, his expression is downcast.

CHARLES
The Scots with Cromwell's new Model army were routing our Northern army.
Do you know what Cromwell says? 'I would rather have a plain russet-coated captain who knows what he fights for, and loves what he knows, than that which you call a gentleman!' His men march singing psalms!
Scarborough Castle was gone. Sandal. Farnham had been desecrated. Oxford. Dear Norfolk's castle at Arundel was

near destroyed. Corfe Castle. Lincoln. More… Great buildings. Castles. It was sacrilege.
How many common people had to die at their hands?
How many of my friends and soldiers?

VIVAS
Was the Queen with you, Sire?

CHARLES
My dear Henrietta was with child. She travelled to the West Country. But fighting broke out in Somerset. Thank God my Queen was able to take a ship from Falmouth and was safe in France with the new baby and the older princes.

The battle of Naseby decided everything.
My Royalists retreated. Cromwell gave chase. My troops surrendered. Five thousand men and five hundred officers were captured. My royal baggage train! All my guns. All the ammunition! Everything.

VIVAS
All lost?

CHARLES
I finally gave myself up. I chose to go with the Scots - to make peace, to keep myself and my family safe.
But agree terms with them? Terms?
'We'll read the English prayer book but no' use it! We'll appoint all army and navy officials! We'll fix our own

terms for parliaments! We'll have Presbyterian Church government. We'll no have Anglican Bishops!'
I am their crowned King - and I have no say!
And when we could not agree, they handed me over to the English Parliamentarians for four hundred thousand pounds! <u>Four hundred thousand pounds!</u>
In God's sweet name, who could I trust?

He turns away up stage.
Pause. Then he swings round to Vivas in a different mood.
Have you been to Hampton Court? I learned tennis there. Racquets. Balls. What a bonnie idea. I am actually quite good at it! I can win!

The English kept me confined at Hampton Court. I could move freely through the house, and occasionally under guard enter the park and glimpse the river Thames - but downstream at St Mary's church in Putney, John Lilburn and his Leveller friends were debating my future with Cromwell.

Vivas leans forward listening hard.
Charles comes down stage to confide in him - it is a secret.
Have you ever smelt danger? Felt it in the air?
They might easily have murdered me at Hampton Court.

Vivas is shocked. He gets to his feet.
VIVAS
Sire, there are paintings. Come! In the Great Hall. You, Sire, on the horse. More. Come.

Charles steps back, surprised. Vivas indicates off stage.

CHARLES

(Still following his own train of thought)

Unexpectedly I had sight of a document left on a hall table at Hampton Court written in an unknown hand...

It is best, it said, for the King to withdraw away from the Army where he would be in such danger. The Isle of Wight would be a good retreat where Colonel Hammond commands. A very honest man...

VIVAS

Sire?

Charles wraps his cloak round himself and puts on his hat.

CHARLES

No one noticed me walking down the central staircase and out across the stone Courtyard. No one would believe I'd abandon my sweet greyhound, that most loyal of subjects. I couldn't look back. Her sacrifice, my leaving her there to fare as she would, gave me time to join five of my most loyal supporters and the horses.

It was too late to think anything but going the way forced on me - and leave the issue to God.

I rode. For my life… for my safety - I rode south. South to the Isle of Wight.

He walks towards Vivas and they exit together, with Vivas leading the way.

CURTAIN

ACT II

Setting: Night. A room in Whitehall. 29th January 1649 - set as Act I

CHARLES enters, wearing hat and cloak.
VIVAS follows at a suitable distance. He carries a lit candle which he places on the table. He retreats to his place again, downstage right.

CHARLES takes off his hat and puts it on the table. He takes off his cloak and drapes it over the chair. He looks confidently out into the audience.

CHARLES
I am King Charles III of Scotland and I am Charles I of England! And that pretty Isle of Wight <u>was</u> England. Colonel Robert Hammond met me at the Quay.
(To Vivas) You've heard of him, I know. He had just then been appointed Governor of the Isle of Wight.

Speaking out into the theatre.
In spite of service to the Parliamentarians, he was a penitent convert to our side. I believed him to be an Independent.
'I will do you all the duty and service in my power, Sire.'
(extending his hand) I gave him my hand to kiss.

He withdraws his hand and puts it over the top of the wine glass on the table for a few seconds, as if to refuse the contents.

CHARLES

Hammond held court in Newport that November morning.
'The King has arrived unexpectedly. I am ordering all Captains of the local Militia to renew their commissions. We want no questioning of your authority to act in any emergency.' And of course, he asked for poultry for my dinner table!
I went in to speak to those gentlemen and received them all graciously.
Not a drop more Christian blood be shed for me, I said, nor am I chargeable to any of you. My one desire is I might dwell here in safety.

(directly to Vivas)

Sir John Oglander - your master - was there. Such a staunch Royalist supporter! And what a great collector of my ship money! There were whispers of what might happen if more of Cromwell's men came to the Island than could be resisted by local people?
And dear Oglander said: 'A boat will convey him away to the mainland.'
The next day I honoured your master with my presence. What a splendid dinner we had at Nunwell. Fifteen courses. Fine local wine. Entertainment. Laughter.
I stayed the night in that part which he now calls The King's Room.

(Speaking out into the theatre again)
It has been said that my going to the Isle of Wight was all contrivance of Cromwell. He wanted me out of the way. In reach of London, but with the Solent as barrier. Maybe he appointed Hammond to entice me away from Hampton Court?

He considers that for a moment, then -

The castle was comfortable enough with rooms for Firebrace, my Page, for my loyal courtiers, Ashburton, Berkeley, Legge - for all my staff… The Great Hall served as my dining hall and sleeping quarters.
Good stables too. My coach was shipped across.
The Island offered me such pleasure.
(He smiles, remembering)
Hunting in Carisbrooke Park. Riding along the Undercliff. I walked through nearby woodland. In Bonchurch, by chance, I attended a very pretty wedding. Another day I was honoured at a banquet in Yarmouth. We rode out and I viewed the Needles.

VIVAS
And in London?

CHARLES takes up the glass and has a gulp of wine.

Pym and Cromwell were already drafting a Treaty. Well, Royal surrender!
Their Commissioners arrived at the castle with the papers for me to consider and sign.

Parliament wants: Control of all the armed forces.
All Royal Proclamations and peerages revoked.
To adjourn any Parliamentary session to a place of their own choosing.

He leans forward to confide Vivas again - it is another secret.
But this was Christmas Eve. The Commissioners went off into Newport to drink and make merry. I had time.
At the side gate and un-noticed, the Scots arrived with a bargain of their own. We worked in secret. No advisors. No servants. Those Scots promised they would raise an army for my delivery and restitution. For it they desired that Presbyterianism be established in England, with political unity between our power base and theirs. I signed.
(Pleased with himself) When the English Commissioners returned, I rejected their demands. They left in fury.

He takes the wine glass back to the table, and picks up his cane.

All this only served to tighten security, put guards at my door and stop any persons approaching me. But Hammond did stand firm against the arrest of the men who conveyed me to this lovely Island.
(To Vivas)
But under constant guard?
Nothing for it but to escape, don't you think?

Speaking out into the theatre again, telling the story.
Sssh! A French ship waits at Southampton. There is a boat ready to carry me to it - if the wind is suitable. I still have

some freedoms. Walks. Visits. Out in the courtyard I look up at the weather vane. The wind is with us. But as I watch it, the wind suddenly changes direction, as if commanded by some unseen force…
And Hammond rides in with fresh orders for the new year. The castle gates close. The guards are doubled. Hammond banishes Ashburton, Berkeley, and Legge too. All my loyal courtiers.

(He beats the floor with his cane) As this dark day proceeds, across the Island children's drums are beating. Women come out on the streets. And with just one musket between them, Island men are shouting, 'For God, the King, and the people.'
'For God, the King, and the people.' 'For God, the King, and the people.'

VIVAS (picking up on the rhythm)
For God, the King, and the people.

CHARLES
As the night closes in, there are ships spread around the Solent to prevent boats from leaving the Island.
In the morning, troops from the Model Army arrive. And more ships come.
Hammond is given immediate powers of Martial Law.

(To Vivas)
There were, I was told, seven ships of the Dutch West India Company off shore that night, fuelling ideas of the Prince of Orange might invade the Isle of Wight.

Captain Burley, the local man who owned the only musket and led the Island uprising, if one might call it so, was tried and executed at Winchester, poor man.

He abandons his cane, and idly picks up the feather pen from the table and fingers the quill.
My letter to the Queen, neatly sewn up into a saddle and sent to Dover, was discovered, they said, by Cromwell himself.
There was a purge of the servants, including my sweet laundry woman Mrs. Wheeler. She did such good service taking secret letters.
Ashburton was still close by. Still faithful. He would carry messages to the mainland.

Letters sent to me were taken! Ones from my dear Henrietta in Holland! And letters from young James, little Henry, and Elizabeth too - three of my poor children, still in England, kept prisoner at St James's palace.

Frustrated, he discards the feather pen onto the table.
Now I could only walk the ramparts of the Castle. Day after day, dreaming of freedom.
A plan. A plan. My kingdom for a plan!

(Confiding in us all) What contrivances we used. Firebrace, my Page of the Bedchamber, would offer his supper to the guard sleeping against my bedchamber door. When the man went for it, Firebrace whispered to me through a hole behind a tapestry...

He leans forward to tell Vivas this story.
Ssh! Ssh!
One by one the castle candles go out.
Can you hear? The courtyard guards are drinking in the gatehouse room. The rope is ready. The window is open.

He suddenly clenches his fists in complete frustration and throws them down against his torso…
No room! No room! How could I have miscalculated the size of that window? How could I?

He pours himself wine and slowly takes a sip.

Good meals. All the comforts. Loyal subjects visiting.
My own failure to escape is in stark contrast to my son James. Dressed as a girl he was spirited away to Holland.
One of us free at least.
There <u>must</u> be a way for me.

VIVAS
My master sent books.

CHARLES
Your master, dear Oglander, called once a week. And yes, he sent me books.
A bowling green was built for me on the eastern bailey of the castle, beyond the curtain wall, within the outer defences. I was learning bowls! If bright weather could be found in such a wet year, Colonel Hammond joined me in the bowling games.

He casts the cloak and cane aside from the chair onto the table. He picks the chair up as he speaks and moves it round ready to climb on it.

Ssh! New plans for escape. I had been moved to an upstairs room in the castle, on the north curtain wall. The window there was high. But Firebrace had removed a bar from the hall window by the staircase. 'Much easier drop, Sire! Creep along the outside wall. We will bribe the two soldiers on the guard platform. Midnight!'
Sshh!

He reaches over the chair and almost climbs onto it. He's showing us - it's not real to him either.
I opened the window and was half out when I saw not two soldiers, but too many - looking my way. I pulled back inside – fast!

He moves the chair smartly back into place, sits down and covers himself with his cloak.

I went straight to bed. I heard musket fire, and the sound of horses retreating. Then Hammond entered my room and after examining that window, bowed.
How now, Hammond, said I. What is the matter? What would you have?
'May it please your Majesty. I have come to take my leave of you, for I hear you are going away?'
Ha! If only!

He discards the cloak and pours the last drop of the wine into the glass.

The civil war raged on - country-wide. Castles besieged! My royalist friends arrested! Wales and Cornwall were holding out - just. Up north the Scots were fighting the English again, but in the end even the Scots were no match for Cromwell.
And there was another Treaty being drawn up to be signed in Newport, with plans for me to stay at the house of Sir William Hopkins.

He drinks and then abandons the glass.
In my last days at Carisbrooke, I met a child on the bowling-green, marching up and down, waving a wooden sword.
What will you do with that terrible weapon? I asked.
'Please, your Majesty, I am going to defend you from your enemies.'
Well, my little friend, I told him, I am going away from here soon, and I do not expect I shall ever return.

He holds his shirt at cravat pin level, remembering.
I patted his head and gave him the gold and ruby ring from my cravat so he might always remember me.
His hand creeps further up his neck. He comes out of that depressing action to look all around him as if in a new world.

(Speaking to Vivas again.)
So, shall I tell you about my time in Newport? Think of it! December, just a few short weeks ago. I was given twenty

days of freedom within the Island. Fine food. Formal gatherings. All show! Freedom? Ha! There were guards at all the doors. I could not go out without escort.

VIVAS
And the Treaty?

CHARLES
There was no real treaty to sign. Just a complete abdication of all my powers.
Your master Oglander was very sceptical. 'We shall have peace, shall we?' said he. 'And the issue of blood will be stopped? And fair weather? And all things according to our own heart's desire?'

VIVAS
There was a jingle they were singing round the town.
'The Time will come, a King cloth'd all in White
Shall crowne this land with Peace in th' Isle of Wight.'
The people know you are innocent.

CHARLES
But nearby, in the George Inn, I could hear the Roundheads and Cavaliers fighting.
(Speaking out into the theatre again.)
The Presbyterians were insisting on a religious settlement in their favour. 'Anglican Bishops for Scotland? Then we will have no King!'
There was other wording I didn't agree with and fought to alter for the country's sake, but Pym's men would have none of it. They are wrong! Wrong!

Days of work in vain. Worse, the murderous Cromwell has marched into Scotland. And the English armoured fleet sailed for Holland to attack the Prince of Wales's ships. My son's fleet!
Cromwell and Pym have purged Parliament of all dissenters. Woe to any man there who speaks in my favour. All my friends are besieged. No one close here will easily serve my escape.
Time runs away like the year end.

In Newport each night – in my so-called freedom at the house of Sir William Hopkins, I dreamt fearful visions - a party of armed men conspiring together to bereave me of my life. Every night.
He picks up his cloak from the chair and pulls it round him for comfort.
It's not a month ago.

(Speaking out into the theatre - but to himself)
Hammond has been ordered to remove me back to Carisbrooke. He has not complied. Now he has been summoned to Windsor.
The wind in Newport is howling. Hear how the rain lashes at the windows?
Firebrace warns me there are soldiers prowling the streets with pistols. 'Two thousand infantry,' he says, 'are suddenly on the Island. This house is bristling with guards.' He and your dear master Oglander want me to try escape.
(Grandly) But that time had past. In the treaty dealings I promised. I am a man of God. And they promised me…

He knocks suddenly and violently on the table.
Vivas jumps.

CHARLES
'Here's knocking indeed!'
Roundhead soldiers force their way into my chamber.
They say I must rise and go with them. They have orders to remove me, they say.
He pulls his cloak closer.

Orders? From whom?
The Army? Remove me, where to?
Hurst?
To Hurst castle?

Vivas reaches out - he can't bear the King to go.
Charles wraps his cloak more formerly, for travelling. He takes up his cane.

CHARLES
Near the coach, dear Firebrace kneels to kiss my hand.
They push him roughly aside.
By Yarmouth Castle, by Henry VIII's Yarmouth Castle, we board. Such a small, insignificant boat. I can see they are playing safe.
(He breathes in deeply as if it's fresh Island air.)
I forsook the English Paradise for this Isle. Now as I leave sweet Wight, it's but another step to heaven.

From the cold comfort confines of Hurst, I go to Windsor. Then to St James.

My day in Parliament is shameful. Not in the House of Commons, this hearing. Oh no! In Westminster Hall! I was crowned in Westminster.

He moves the chair to the centre facing the audience and sits down in it, cloak and cane and all - reliving the moment.

Only the chosen few sit in judgement. An illegal court chosen by the 'Rump' parliament - rump if ever I saw it. And <u>so</u> few of them. Only sixty or so are here. No one I know. No friends. No supporters.

He looks up at 'someone' standing stage left beside him.

The Solicitor General John Cook stands and starts to read the indictment.
Hold!
Hold, I say!
He rises angrily from the chair.
Hold!

He strikes out 'at Cook' with his cane. The cane drops out of his hand.
He looks in both directions expecting someone to retrieve it. No one does. (Not even Vivas because it's part of telling the story.) Charles has to pick it up himself. Concerned now, he retreats, but still with some grandeur, to the chair.

I sit silent. They call me tyrant, traitor and murderer. Public and implacable enemy to the Commonwealth of England. They accuse me of wicked design to erect and uphold an unlimited and tyrannical power to rule according to my will. To overthrow the rights and liberties of the people of England. The army proclaims me to be a man of blood.
'How do you plead?' Cook says.

Charles rises righteously from the chair.
How do I plead? No court has jurisdiction over the monarch. My authority is by Divine Right, given to me by God, and sanctified by the traditions and laws of England when I was anointed and crowned. I would know by what power I am called hither? By what authority - and I mean lawful authority? The House of Commons, on its own, cannot try anybody. I refuse to plead.

VIVAS
You are the King!

CHARLES
Yes! But thirty witnesses are summoned. Their evidence is heard in the Painted Chamber, not in Westminster Hall. I am not allowed to hear what is said against me. And given no opportunity to question it. Two days of debate without me. I am guilty, they say. They refuse to hear me speak. At a public session - just three days ago - they read out the sentence to the packed gallery: This court being satisfied that he, Charles Stuart, is guilty of the crimes of which

he has been accused, do judge him tyrant, traitor, murderer, and public enemy to the good people of the nation, to be put to death by the severing of his head from his body.
Hhmmaaah! *(Realisation of horror)*

Vivas turns away and momentarily covers his ears - he can't bear to hear it.

CHARLES
And finally I am bundled here to Whitehall - to this banqueting house dear Inigo Jones built.

He picks up the wine flagon.
SHOUTS from off stage right.
Charles looks up towards it. Vivas looks up too.

CHARLES
They come for me. Dawn - and I've not slept.
(pause)
There will be time enough for that.
(pause)
(looking at Vivas)
Vivas. Such a Spanish name? Has it brought you luck?

VIVAS
It means 'sail' also. My grandfather was shipwrecked off the Needles in 1558.

CHARLES
Ah! The Armada!

(Drawing up very straight.)
I have the heart and stomach of a King, and a King of England too!
(To Vivas - almost as a warning) I have trusted you. Remember!

Vivas puts his hand to his heart.

Charles pauses, then up-ends the wine flagon over the glass. The flagon is empty.

CHARLES
'The wine of life is drawn.'

He abandons the flagon and begins to remove his cloak.
Vivas rises and stands watching him.

CHARLES
I am directly descended from Mary Queen of Scots. My father was James VI in Scotland as well as James I of England. I am King Charles III of Scotland and I am King Charles I of England! All my days I have tried to do the right thing for my country. For my people.

He removes his waistcoat and puts it neatly on the table. He places the cane beside it. He takes up the bible.

(Directly to Vivas)
I go now!
Give my true friend Sir John Oglander my grateful thanks.

Vivas bows very deeply.

CHARLES
The morning will be cold. I will wear two shirts. I will not face death with my people thinking I shiver because I am afraid. I go to my God with all Sovereign dignity, and in full expectation of the life to come.

He turns towards stage right.
Suddenly, he turns urgently back towards Vivas and reaches out.
He points off stage left.

CHARLES
Do not forget! Take my little Spaniel!

Facing the audience, he presses the bible tightly to his chest, and to himself - almost whispering
God, sweet God, save your King.

Charles turns and exits through the doors stage right, head held high.

Vivas clutches his cloak tightly round him and stands very still for several seconds, watching Charles go.
A short mournful howl of a dog. Vivas hears it and exits stage left.

The candle on the table goes out.

CURTAIN

FURNITURE AND PROPERTY LIST

ACT I

On stage:
A round table: *On it:*

Bible.
Quill pen.
Scroll of paper.
Ornate wine glass.
Charles's Hat

Vivas enters with a **flagon of wine** and places it on downstage side of the table.

Grand wooden chair: *leaning against it:* Walking Cane

Hanging: Portraits of James I, Mary Queen of Scots, Queen Elizabeth I

Personal: **Charles** Cloak, the hat.

ACT II

On stage:
A round table: *On it:*

Bible.
Quill pen.
Scroll of paper.
Large flagon of wine.
Ornate wine glass.

Vivas enters with a **lit candle** and places it on downstage side of the table.

Grand wooden chair: *leaning against it:* Walking Cane

Hanging: Portraits of James I, Mary Queen of Scots, Queen Elizabeth I

Personal: **Charles** Cloak, the hat.

LIGHTING PLOT

Property fittings required:
Candle (battery operated and remote controlled)
1 interior setting.

ACT I

To open: Night.

(Page 3)
Some general lighting
Window (created by lighting off stage left) - shafts of moonlight - or glow of street lamp.

Cue 1 (Page 29)
Charles walks towards Vivas and they exit together, with Vivas leading the way.

CURTAIN

ACT II

(Page 30)

Same general lighting as ACT I
Vivas enters with a lit candle. He places it in the centre of the table.

Cue 1 (Page 43)

Begin to add soft pink light of early dawn from the window as Charles speaks:

Charles ...

Thirty witnesses are summoned. Their evidence is heard in the Painted Chamber, not in Westminster Hall. I am not allowed to hear what is said against me. And given no opportunity to question it. Two days of debate without me. I am guilty, they say. They refuse to hear me speak....

Cue 2 (Page 46)

Charles turns and exits through the doors stage right, head held high. Vivas clutches his cloak tightly round him and stands very still for several seconds, watching Charles go.

SOUND *A short mournful* ***HOWL*** *of a dog.*

Then Vivas exits stage left.

Go to Black

Brief Pause.

The candle on the table goes out.

CURTAIN

QUOTATIONS

'What watch the King keeps to maintain the peace.'
Page 16
Shakespeare: Henry V Act IV Scene 1

'This earth of majesty, this seat of Mars…'
Page 17
Shakespeare: Richard II Act II Scene 1

'Tis not the balm, the sceptre, and the ball…'
Page 18
Shakespeare: Henry V Act IV Scene 1

'Oh Scotland... Scotland.'
Page 22
Shakespeare: Macbeth Act IV Scene 3

I wept 'for joy to stand upon my kingdom once again…'
Page 26
Shakespeare: Richard II Act III Scene 2

'Here's knocking indeed!'
Page 41
Shakespeare Macbeth Act II Scene 3

'The wine of life is drawn.'
Page 45
Shakespeare: Macbeth Act II Scene 3

The Royal Line

Elizabeth of York - as the wife of Henry VII she was the first Tudor queen. Daughter of Edward IV and niece of Richard III, she married Henry following his victory at the Battle of Bosworth - the last phase of the Wars of the Roses. She was the mother of King Henry VIII.
Margaret Tudor eldest daughter of Henry VII and Elizabeth of York, and sister of Henry VIII, married James IV of Scotland.

Their son became James V King of Scotland until his death following the Scottish defeat at the Battle of Solway Moss. His only surviving legitimate child, Mary, born two weeks after he died, succeeded him when she was just six days old.

Mary Queen of Scots was sent as a child to France, later to be married to the Dauphin of France. He ascended the French throne as King Francis II in 1559, and Mary briefly became queen consort of France. Widowed after only one year, Mary returned to Scotland as Queen. Four years later, she married her first cousin, Lord Darnley who was later murdered. Mary's son by Lord Darnley became James VI of Scotland. When Queen Elizabeth I died leaving no heir, James also became James I of England.

Charles I was the second son of James and ascended the throne of the Three Kingdoms - England, Scotland and Ireland in 1625.
Charles married Henrietta Maria of France, daughter of Henri IV, and sister of Louis XIII of France

The children of Charles I

Charles - afterwards Charles II.

Mary - afterwards Princess of Orange and mother of William III - William of Orange.

James, Duke of York - afterwards James II.

Elizabeth - died aged 14 at Carisbrooke Castle - buried in St Thomas's Church Newport Isle of Wight.

Henrietta Anne - married the Duke of Orleans.

The sister of Charles I, Elizabeth Stuart married Frederick, Elector of Palantine - briefly Queen of Bohemia until that throne was lost and they fled to Holland. With the demise of the Stuart dynasty in 1714, Elizabeth's grandson succeeded to the British throne as George I of Great Britain, initiating the Hanover line of succession. Elizabeth II is Elizabeth Stuart's direct descendant of the 10th and 11th generation through different paths.

Other books by Felicity Fair Thompson

www.felicityfair.co.uk

Cutting In

Ambition can take over your life. Ballet is no ordinary career for Elaine, more a magnificent obsession. Insecure and unloved, she is desperate to prove herself. Watching the beautiful Beverley dance, Elaine imitates, borrows, steals, wanting everything Beverley has. Each movement. Every reaction. Each smile. To stalk in pursuit of an image. There's no threat in that, surely? Eighteen, it's a dangerous age, when a girl has to cut her way into life.

One of the three top finalists in the Beryl Bainbridge Award, People's Book Prize 2012/13

'Hard edged, striking and truthful.'
Best selling novelist Julian Rathbone
'Poignant and believable.'
Averil Ashfield, Transworld Books
'A great gift for portraying the agonies and ecstasies of adolescence. A rare talent.'
Frederick E Smith, Best Selling Novelist and Screen Writer
'I read it at a single sitting. Perceptive writing wonderfully spiked with bitchiness.'
Graham Hurley, Crime Writer

Published by Wight Diamond Press
0-9535123-0-4

Hold Tight

A wall of window high up. The child watches the night close in, several times huffing against the glass to mist it up, pressing her hand into the condensation and watching the imprint slowly fade.

When a small child is abducted, WPC Jane Velalley shares the long cruel hours of waiting with the distraught mother. With her own home life in turmoil, and facing escalating criminal activity and emotional distress, Velalley must use all her energy and wits, and still hold tight to everything she loves and values most herself.

'Unputdownable! A novel and screenplay rolled into one. It had me on the edge of my seat. Fantastic!'
Michelle Magorian Author of' Goodnight Mister Tom'
'Gripping and emotional read, I couldn't put it down.'
Writer Mary Grand
'Beautifully crafted. Really perceptive descriptions.'
D.M. Australia
'A well crafted, emotional novel.'
Writer Lucy Blanchard
'Written with enormous sensitivity but never flinching from challenging issues, the plot weaves its way deftly through this societal minefield…You're terrified…but unable to look away.
Hold Tight is compelling reading.'
Gill Kay, Editor Ingenue Magazine

Published by Wight Diamond Press
978-0-9535123-3-1

The Kid on Slapton Beach

Children all over the world are caught up in wars. So many people have to leave their homes and everything they know behind.
The tank by the Ley at Torcross in Devon is real. In World War II Exercise Tiger is historic fact.

War is hard enough when your Dad is missing in action, and even harder when you have to leave everything you know and love.
Twelve year old Harry is one of three thousand people leaving the coast in Devon in the Second World War as U.S. troops move into the area, planning secret D-Day rehearsals on the beach there in April 1944.
But what if your most treasured possession is left behind?

'Superb on so many levels... a wonderful book.'
Michelle Magorian Author of 'Goodnight Mister Tom'
'A great read that rushes to a brilliant climax!'
John Ovenden ABC Broadcaster and Journalist Australia
'...a pivotal moment in the war...'
Joint Forces Journal USA
'A great story and very well told.'
Anna Home Chair of the Children's Film and Television Foundation
'This book is beautiful. A jewel!'
Actress June Brown, Dot in East Enders.

Published by Wight Diamond Press
978-0-9535123-2-4

www.ingramcontent.com/pod-product-compliance
Ingram Content Group UK Ltd.
Pitfield, Milton Keynes, MK11 3LW, UK
UKHW042009190726
13854UKWH00005B/2225

9 781789 552119